United States General Accounting Office

GAO

Report to Congressional Committees

I0425890

March 2003

WORLD TRADE ORGANIZATION

First-Year U.S. Efforts to Monitor China's Compliance

GAO
Accountability ★ Integrity ★ Reliability

GAO-03-461

Highlights

Highlights of GAO-03-461, a report to the Chairman and the Ranking Minority Member, Senate Committee on Finance, and to the Chairman and the Ranking Minority Member, House Committee on Ways and Means

WORLD TRADE ORGANIZATION

First-Year U.S. Efforts to Monitor China's Compliance

Why GAO Did This Study

China's December 2001 membership in the World Trade Organization created substantial opportunities for U.S. companies seeking to expand into China's vast market, and for significant reforms within China at all levels of government. However, the benefits of China's membership in the World Trade Organization are contingent on China's successful implementation of its commitments. In recognizing this fact, Congress has provided increased resources to executive branch agencies to enhance the government's ability to effectively monitor and enforce China's compliance. In this study, one of several that GAO will conduct for Congress on China-World Trade Organization issues, GAO was asked to (1) examine key agencies' organizational changes and the interagency process used to carry out compliance responsibilities and (2) review how the agencies have addressed compliance issues that arose during the first year of China's membership, by using two specific examples; the examples illustrate the type of compliance issues U.S. officials face but are not representative of China's compliance record overall.

The U.S. Trade Representative and other agency officials provided technical and editorial comments mainly on our characterization of issues relating to tariff-rate quotas and the multilateral review of China's trade policies. We clarified these issues and made other changes as appropriate.

www.gao.gov/cgi-bin/getrpt?GAO-03-461.

To view the full report, including the scope and methodology, click on the link above. For more information, contact Susan Westin at (202) 512-4128 or westins@gao.gov.

What GAO Found

In order to better monitor China's compliance with its World Trade Organization commitments, the U.S. Trade Representative and the departments of Agriculture, Commerce, and State have

- reorganized or established intra-agency teams to coordinate their oversight of China's compliance;
- increased staff from about 28 to 53 in key units in Washington, D.C., and China from fiscal year 2000 to 2002; and
- reflected these changes in their agencies' recent performance and strategic plans.

In addition, the U.S. Trade Representative is leading a new interagency working group on China's compliance to identify, analyze, and resolve problems. This group, which utilizes private sector input, was very active in monitoring and responding to issues during the first year of China's membership, although it took some time for agencies to work out their respective roles and responsibilities in the interagency group.

U.S. agencies' experiences in two areas during the first year of China's World Trade Organization membership illustrate the challenges ahead in addressing compliance issues. First, problems regarding China's commitments to grant market access to certain bulk agricultural commodities through the use of tariff-rate quotas show the extensive effort required to identify difficulties, gather and analyze information, and begin to resolve complex and technical issues with China. Second, disagreement among World Trade Organization members over how to conduct a comprehensive annual review of China's trade policies within the World Trade Organization led to a limited first-year review that did not meet U.S. expectations, and illustrated the challenges of gaining consensus in this multilateral forum to improve future oversight. Problems in both of these areas are unresolved, and U.S. officials continue to pursue their resolution with China in 2003.

Many Actors Monitor China's World Trade Organization Compliance

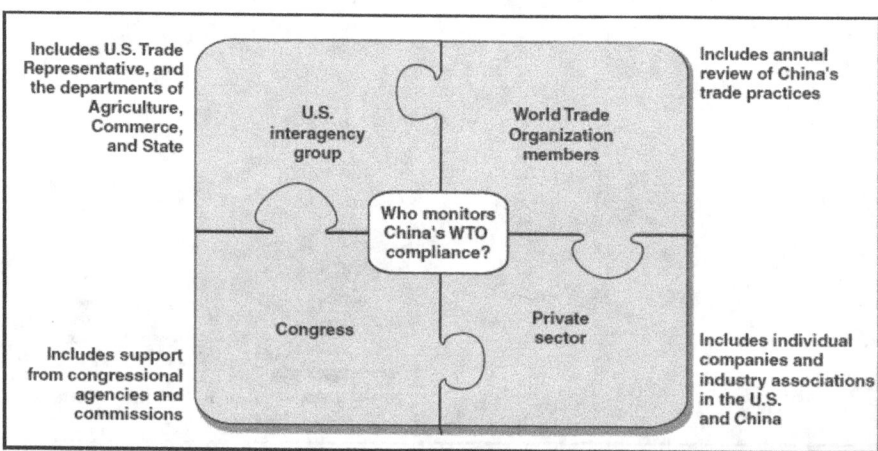

Source: GAO.

Contents

Abbreviations

FAS	Foreign Agricultural Service
FCS	Foreign Commercial Service
MOFTEC	Ministry of Foreign Trade and Economic Cooperation
SPDC	State Development and Planning Commission
USDA	U.S. Department of Agriculture
USTR	U.S. Trade Representative
TRIPS	Trade-related Aspects of Intellectual Property Rights
TRM	Transitional Review Mechanism
TRQ	Tariff-rate Quota
WTO	World Trade Organization

United States General Accounting Office
Washington, D.C. 20548

March 31, 2003

The Honorable Charles E. Grassley
Chairman
The Honorable Max Baucus
Ranking Minority Member
Committee on Finance
United States Senate

The Honorable William M. Thomas
Chairman
The Honorable Charles B. Rangel
Ranking Minority Member
Committee on Ways and Means
House of Representatives

China's accession to the World Trade Organization in December 2001 signified that the U.S.'s fourth largest trading partner would be subject to the multilateral organization's requirements to liberalize its trade. By joining the World Trade Organization, China committed to adhere to the principles of a rules-based global trading system and give foreign goods and services greater access to its markets. U.S. officials have recognized that the benefits of these comprehensive commitments are contingent on China's fulfilling its obligations. Recognizing that monitoring and enforcement of the commitments specified in China's accession agreement would be of great importance, Congress enacted legislation to ensure such oversight.[1]

As part of your request for us to undertake a long-term body of work related to China's membership in the World Trade Organization, we reviewed how the U.S. Trade Representative, the Department of Commerce, the Department of Agriculture, and the Department of State are positioned to monitor and enforce China's compliance with its commitments. Specifically, in this report we (1) describe the changes to each agency's organization, resources, and plans in light of China's accession, and to the interagency process used to fulfill these responsibilities; and (2) review how these agencies have addressed certain compliance issues that have arisen during the first year of China's World Trade Organization membership.

---

[1]Pub. L. 106-286, 114 Stat. 901 (Oct. 10, 2000).

In order to perform our review, we studied the agencies' budget and staffing information, performance and strategic planning documents, and other official documentation and reports relating to the agencies' efforts to monitor and enforce China's compliance with its commitments. We supplemented this information by reviewing World Trade Organization documents and by interviewing knowledgeable U.S., foreign government, and World Trade Organization officials and private sector representatives. To analyze how the United States has addressed compliance issues, we examined two areas of China's commitments. First, we chose to examine activities related to China's regulating imports of certain bulk agricultural commodities (such as corn and cotton) because the area was economically important to U.S. exporters, China made extensive commitments to change its practices, and significant monitoring and enforcement activity occurred in the first year of China's World Trade Organization membership. Second, we chose to examine activities that related to implementing a comprehensive annual review of China's trade policies within the World Trade Organization, because the area concerned issues that were important to U.S. officials, including Congress, and conducting the review is an important aspect of World Trade Organization members' ability to monitor and enforce Chinese compliance. These two areas are not representative of China's compliance record overall but do illustrate the kinds of compliance issues that U.S. officials try to resolve.[2] (See app. I for details on our scope and methodology.)

Results in Brief

China's accession to the World Trade Organization led to increased monitoring and enforcement responsibilities for the U.S. government. In response to these increased responsibilities, the U.S. Trade Representative and the departments of Commerce, Agriculture, and State have undertaken various efforts to enhance their ability to monitor China's compliance with its World Trade Organization commitments. For example, the agencies have reorganized or established intra-agency teams to improve the coordination of their monitoring and enforcement efforts. Additionally, the

---

[2]The U.S. Trade Representative's first report to Congress on China's World Trade Organization compliance noted that overall in 2002 China made significant progress in implementing its commitments, both in undertaking many of the required systemic changes and in implementing specific commitments. At the same time, the report noted serious concerns in some areas where implementation had not yet occurred or was inadequate. See U.S. Trade Representative, 2002 Report to Congress on China's WTO Compliance (Washington, D.C.: Office of the U.S. Trade Representative, Dec. 11, 2002).

agencies have added staff in Washington, D.C., and overseas in China to carry out these efforts. For example, estimated full-time equivalent staff in key units that are involved in China monitoring and enforcement activities across the four agencies increased from about 28 to 53 from fiscal year 2000 to 2002, with the largest increases at the Department of Commerce. The agencies' recent strategic and planning documents also reflect an emphasis on China trade compliance efforts. On a broader level, the U.S. Trade Representative has established an interagency group to coordinate U.S. government compliance activities. The interagency group, which utilizes the private sector to support its efforts, was very active in monitoring and responding to issues during the first year of China's membership, although it took some time for agencies to work out their respective roles and responsibilities in the interagency group.

Monitoring and enforcement of China's compliance with World Trade Organization requirements is a complex and challenging task, as shown by the U.S.'s experience in two areas during 2002: examining China's regulation of imports of bulk agricultural commodities and participating in an annual multilateral review of China's trade practices. In the first area we reviewed, China's commitments related to its importing bulk agricultural commodities, implementation problems that arose in 2002 included concerns about Chinese authorities missing deadlines for issuing tariff-rate quotas on commodities; disagreement over whether China's interpretation of its commitments met World Trade Organization requirements; and questions about whether new Chinese administrative practices are in keeping with China's obligations. The United States has undertaken both bilateral and multilateral activities to settle these complex issues, which have yet to be resolved. The large number of U.S. government activities in this area, which included at least monthly engagement with China, illustrates the extensive effort agencies must undertake to identify problems, gather and analyze information, and respond to some issues. In the second area we reviewed, the U.S. experience implementing a comprehensive annual review of China's trade practices within the World Trade Organization shows the challenge of achieving multilateral support and consensus on an issue. Disagreement among World Trade Organization members over implementing commitments creating this "transitional review mechanism" limited the World Trade Organization's multilateral oversight of China's compliance in 2002. The first review of China's trade practices did not meet the initial expectations of U.S. officials with regard to the thoroughness of the review. They also expressed disappointment over the results of the review, which failed to produce a final report or recommendations to improve future implementation because there was no consensus to do so among WTO members, including China. However, U.S. officials cited benefits from participating in the World Trade Organization review process, such as demonstrating to China the United States' commitment to thoroughly reviewing China's World Trade Organization implementation, and solidifying interagency coordination for the years ahead. U.S. officials also said they will work with China and other World Trade Organization members to establish more workable procedures for future reviews, and that they were hopeful that the process will be improved over the next 9 years that the review is scheduled to be conducted.

Background

China became the 143rd member of the World Trade Organization (WTO) on December 11, 2001, after almost 15 years of negotiations. These negotiations resulted in China's commitments to open and liberalize its economy and offer a more predictable environment for trade and foreign investment in accordance with WTO rules. The United States and other WTO members have stated that China's membership in the WTO provides increased opportunities for foreign companies seeking access to China's vast market. China is already a major destination of U.S. investment overseas, and total trade between China and the United States was an estimated $145 billion in 2002, based on U.S. trade data.

The U.S. government's efforts to ensure China's compliance with its WTO commitments are part of an overall U.S. structure to monitor and enforce foreign governments' compliance with existing trade agreements.[3] At least 17 federal agencies, led by the Office of the U.S. Trade Representative (USTR), are involved in these overall monitoring and enforcement activities. USTR and the departments of Agriculture (USDA), Commerce, and State have relatively broad roles and primary responsibilities with respect to trade agreement monitoring and enforcement. Other agencies, such as the departments of the Treasury and Labor, play more specialized roles. Federal monitoring and enforcement efforts are coordinated through an interagency mechanism comprised of several management- and staff-level committees and subcommittees. The congressional structure for funding and overseeing federal monitoring and enforcement activities is

---

[3]For more information on the overall roles and responsibilities of U.S. government agencies in monitoring and enforcing trade agreements, see U.S. General Accounting Office, *International Trade: Strategy Needed to Better Monitor and Enforce Trade Agreements*, GAO/NSIAD-00-76 (Washington, D.C.: Mar. 14, 2000).

also complex, because it involves multiple committees of jurisdiction. Congressional agencies and commissions also support Congress's oversight on China-WTO trade issues. In addition to the executive branch and congressional structures, multiple private sector advisory committees exist to provide federal agencies with policy and technical advice on trade matters, including trade agreement monitoring and enforcement.

Key Agencies Have Increased Focus on China WTO Compliance and Coordinate Efforts through an Interagency Process

In response to the increased responsibilities arising from China's accession to the WTO, USTR, Commerce, USDA, and State have undertaken various efforts to increase their ability to monitor China's compliance with its WTO commitments. On an intra-agency level, each of the four agencies have reorganized or established teams to better coordinate the activities among the various agency units involved in China WTO compliance. Additionally, the agencies have devoted additional staff resources in Washington, D.C., and China to enhance their monitoring and enforcement efforts. The agencies' recent performance and strategic planning documents also reflect this increased emphasis on monitoring and enforcement. In addition to the efforts of the individual agencies, USTR established a staff-level interagency working group focused on China WTO compliance to identify, analyze, and resolve problems. Businesses and industry associations support the U.S. government's efforts by providing information on Chinese trade practices, alerting the government to market access problems, and providing input on policy issues.

Agencies Have Made Organizational Changes to Facilitate China WTO Compliance Efforts

To enhance coordination on China WTO compliance issues, USTR has reorganized by merging two offices, while Commerce, State, and USDA have established intra-agency teams. Each of the agencies we reviewed includes within their organizational structures an office that focuses exclusively on China or the greater Asian region. These offices have the primary responsibility for coordinating the agencies' China WTO compliance efforts, but other units in the agencies are routinely involved. Coordination with these units generally includes obtaining input from and sharing information with specialists in other offices on China trade issues, communicating with agency staff in the field overseas, participating in the interagency process of reviewing China's WTO compliance, and coordinating with other governments and private sector representatives.

USTR

USTR's recent reorganization responds to the new responsibilities arising from China's membership in the WTO. USTR created an Office of North Asian Affairs in June 2002 by merging the Office of China and the Office of Japan; the office has primary responsibility for coordinating the agency's efforts on China WTO trade issues.[4] According to USTR, the reorganization reflected a shift in the agency's activities resulting from China's accession to the WTO and enables the agency to make the best possible use of its resources to maintain a high level of attention to trading partners in the region.

The Office of General Counsel and other sector- and function-specific offices within USTR continue to support the Office of North Asian Affairs on China trade issues by providing subject matter or other specialized expertise.[5] Additionally, USTR's Monitoring and Enforcement Unit within the Office of General Counsel would have primary responsibility for representing the United States if a China-related dispute settlement case were brought before the WTO. Moreover, the USTR office in Geneva, Switzerland, represents U.S. interests in proceedings at the WTO.

Department of Commerce

Commerce created an intra-agency China Compliance Team in May 2001 (in anticipation of China's accession to the WTO) to facilitate the agency's compliance efforts, which are related to industrial goods and services. Staff from six[6] Commerce units comprise the team, which is chaired by the Executive Director of Commerce's Market Access and Compliance division.[7] The team meets twice weekly to share information among the

---

[4]An Assistant U.S. Trade Representative heads the office, which has overall responsibility for overseeing trade policy toward China, Japan, Hong Kong, South Korea, Mongolia, and Taiwan.

[5]In some cases, these offices take the lead on certain China trade issues. For example, USTR's Office of Services, Investment, and Intellectual Property has the lead role on China-related intellectual property issues, such as monitoring China's compliance with WTO rules on enforcing patent and trademark protection. However, the office coordinates with the Office of North Asian Affairs to ensure information sharing between the two units.

[6]Besides Market Access and Compliance, the other offices that comprise the China Compliance Team are Import Administration, Trade Development, U.S. and Foreign Commercial Service (FCS), the Trade Information Center, and the Office of General Counsel.

[7]Within Market Access and Compliance, two offices, the Office of China Economic Area and the Trade Compliance Center, are directly involved in coordinating the agency's China compliance activities on most issues.

various offices and coordinate the agency's position and actions on China's implementation of its WTO commitments.

USDA

Shortly after China's accession to the WTO in December 2001, USDA recognized the need to gather expertise from across the agency to aid in effectively monitoring China's WTO compliance regarding agriculture. As a result, USDA created two intra-agency task forces—a USDA-wide task force and a working-level task force within USDA's Foreign Agricultural Service (FAS). Six USDA agencies participate in the USDA-wide China Task Force, which was created in February 2002 and meets quarterly. The FAS-wide China Task Force, which was first convened in March 2002, meets monthly to develop strategies for resolving China compliance issues.[8] FAS officials said that both task forces are an effective means of sharing information and ensuring that the technical expertise of all relevant units are taken into consideration when responding to a compliance issue.[9]

Department of State

Following China's accession to the WTO, State officers at the U.S. embassy in Beijing took the lead in coordinating the U.S. government's compliance efforts in China. To that end, the embassy established a WTO Implementation Coordination Committee, which meets monthly and is chaired by the embassy's economic minister. The committee coordinates the embassy's WTO monitoring, compliance, technical assistance, and outreach efforts. State officers from relevant sections, as well as overseas officers from Commerce, USDA, and Customs, comprise the committee. According to State, the committee plays an important role in gathering, summarizing, and communicating information from China to U.S. government agencies in Washington, D.C.[10]

At State headquarters, the Office of Chinese and Mongolian Affairs serves as the main communications link between U.S. agencies in Washington, D.C., and the U.S. embassy and consulates general in China. The office is

---

[8]Within FAS, the Asia and the Americas Division and the Multilateral Trade Negotiations Division have direct responsibility for coordinating the agency's China WTO compliance efforts. These two divisions coordinate with other FAS units to obtain input and expertise on specific agricultural commodities and other technical issues. For example, staff in FAS commodity-specific units analyze and provide input on China's regulations relating to biotechnology and sanitary measures.

[9]Both task forces may convene more frequently if the need arises.

[10]The embassy has also established a working group specifically focused on monitoring China's intellectual property legislation and enforcement.

therefore responsible for coordinating instructions and other diplomatic dispatches to the posts on China WTO compliance issues. This office coordinates with offices in State's Bureau of Economic and Business Affairs to obtain sector-specific and other technical expertise on China trade issues.

Agencies Have Allocated Additional Resources to China Monitoring and Enforcement Efforts

USTR, Commerce, USDA, and State have requested and received additional resources to carry out the additional responsibilities arising from China's accession to the WTO. For example, full-time equivalent staff in key units that are involved in China monitoring and enforcement activities across the four agencies increased from about 28 to 53 from fiscal year 2000 to 2002, based on agency officials' estimates (see table 1). Congress's October 2000 legislation authorizing the President to grant permanent normal trade relations status to China contained specific provisions authorizing the appropriation of additional resources for monitoring and enforcement efforts at agencies' headquarters and on the ground in China.[11] Although no appropriation has been made under that October 2000 legislation, the President's fiscal year 2001 budget requested $22 million for the four agencies to fund a Trade Compliance Initiative that emphasized the need for resources to monitor WTO compliance. Subsequently, Congress appropriated funds for the agencies' overall monitoring and enforcement efforts, a portion of which the agencies used to enhance China compliance efforts.

---

[11]Pub. L. 106-286, § 413, 114 Stat. 901.

Table 1: Agency Staffing Estimates for Key Offices Involved in China WTO Compliance Efforts, Fiscal Years 2000-2002

Agency	2000	2001	2002
USTR	3	3	5
Commerce			
Market Access and Compliance[a]	7	19	22
Import Administration[b]	1.7	3.3	6.7
USDA			
Asia and the Americas Division [c]	2.5	2.5	2.5
FAS China field offices (excluding Hong Kong)	5	5	8
State			
Office of Chinese and Mongolian Affairs[d]	2.25	2.25	3.25
Beijing embassy economic section[e]	6	6	5.5
Total	**27.5**	**41.1**	**53**

Sources: USTR, Commerce, USDA, and State estimates for fiscal years 2000-2002.

Note: Totals do not add due to rounding.

[a]Figures for Market Access and Compliance include actual full-time staff in the Office of China Economic Area, the Trade Compliance Center, and members of a Rapid Response trade compliance team who focus on China. The figure for 2002 does not include two overseas compliance officers that were approved in 2001, but were not placed until the end of fiscal year 2002 and early fiscal year 2003.

[b]With the exception of officers posted overseas in China, Import Administration officers do not have country-specific work portfolios. Therefore, these figures are based on Import Administration's estimates of actual full-time equivalent staff working on China compliance issues. These figures do not include staff who conduct antidumping proceedings involving imports from China.

[c]Figures for the Asia and the Americas Division are based on FAS estimates of actual full-time equivalent staff working on China compliance issues.

[d]Figures for the Office of Chinese and Mongolian affairs are based on State's estimates of actual full-time equivalent staff in the unit's economic section, which is the section that is most involved in China WTO compliance issues.

[e]Figures for the Beijing embassy economic section are based on State's estimates of actual full-time equivalent staff working on China compliance issues.

Commerce had the largest overall increase in staff devoted to China WTO compliance. Specifically, staffing levels in Commerce's Market Access and Compliance division increased from 7 to 22 between fiscal years 2000 and 2002. Additionally, Commerce's Import Administration, which takes the lead on monitoring China's commitments concerning subsidies and unfair trade practices, also significantly increased staff dedicated to China compliance activities over the same time period.[12] Commerce has also increased the number of staff involved in agency's compliance efforts on the ground in China by creating a Trade Facilitation Office within the Beijing embassy.[13] In fiscal year 2001, Commerce established positions in this office for two Market Access and Compliance officers and two Import Administration officers. However, the positions were not filled until the end of fiscal year 2002 and early fiscal year 2003 due to training and delays in obtaining security clearances for the staff. According to Commerce, the office works with industry representatives to identify and address market access and WTO compliance concerns. USDA has also increased the number of overseas staff involved in the agency's China WTO compliance activities. Specifically, FAS added a senior policy agricultural attaché to the embassy in Beijing and added two officers at the Agricultural Trade Offices in Beijing and Shanghai in fiscal year 2002.[14] Attachés at the embassy are most directly involved in implementing the agency's efforts to oversee China's WTO compliance with its agriculture commitments. FAS officials said that other overseas officers play a critical role in tracking China's compliance through their contacts with Chinese officials and traders in China. For example, officers in the Agricultural Trade Offices track agriculture-related laws and regulations issued by the Chinese government and communicate this information to headquarters staff.

---

[12]Import Administration's responsibilities include enforcing U.S. law relating to antidumping measures and countervailing duties. Antidumping measures include a duty or fee imposed to neutralize the injurious effect of unfair pricing practices known as "dumping." Dumping refers to the sale of a commodity in a foreign market at a lower price than its normal market value. A countervailing duty is a special duty that an importing country imposes to offset the economic effect of a subsidy and to prevent injury to a domestic industry caused by a subsidized import.

[13]U.S. and Foreign Commercial Service (FCS) officers in five locations throughout China (Beijing, Chengdu, Guangzhou, Shanghai, and Shenyang) also support Commerce's in-country compliance and monitoring efforts by maintaining contact with U.S. companies in China and gathering information about potential compliance problems.

[14]A third Agricultural Trade Office is located in Guangzhou.

Agency Performance and Strategic Planning Documents Reflect Emphasis on China WTO Compliance Issues

In addition to making organizational changes and devoting additional resources to China WTO compliance efforts, the key agencies have also identified monitoring and enforcement as a priority in the agencies' recent planning documents.[15] For example, USTR specifically added China WTO monitoring and enforcement as a key agency performance goal in the agency's fiscal year 2003 performance plan and most recent strategic plan. Additionally, State's 2003 Mission Performance Plan for the overseas posts in China added specific goals, actions, and strategies related to the posts' roles in monitoring and assisting in the enforcement of China's WTO commitments.[16] And although the most recent Commerce and USDA planning documents do not include specific goals relating to China WTO compliance, the plans do include more general goals relating to the monitoring and enforcement of existing WTO agreements. Both of these agencies' plans also set forth broad strategies for ensuring market access for U.S. companies.

New Interagency Group Coordinates Compliance Activities and Utilizes Private Sector to Support Efforts

U.S. government agencies coordinate their monitoring and enforcement activities through a formal interagency process and structure that is intended to ensure that the development of trade policy reflects a range of agency perspectives.[17] Within this overall structure, a newly established multiagency, staff-level group focuses on China's compliance with its WTO commitments. The agencies also seek input from businesses and industry groups for support on compliance activities.

---

[15]The Government Performance and Results Act of 1993, Pub. L. 103-62, requires federal agencies to engage in a results-oriented strategic planning process. In general, the plans include descriptions of agency goals and objectives, and measures for assessing the agency's performance in meeting those goals.

[16]Mission Performance Plans are annual embassy plans describing performance goals and objectives.

[17]Congress created an interagency structure in the Trade Expansion Act of 1962, codified at 19 U.S.C. §1872, which has been amended several times. This structure, called the Trade Policy Committee, led by USTR, has two subordinate bodies–the Trade Policy Review Group (a management-level committee) and the Trade Policy Staff Committee (a senior staff-level committee subordinate to the management-level committee). These subordinate committees include all the agencies that are members of the Trade Policy Committee, as well as a wide range of other agencies.

Interagency Group Focuses on China WTO Compliance

In 2001, USTR created an interagency group whose mandate is devoted exclusively to monitoring China and the extent to which it is complying with its WTO commitments.[18] USTR's Office of North Asian Affairs is responsible for chairing this new Trade Policy Staff Committee, Subcommittee on China WTO Compliance. Almost 40 officials, representing 14 departments and executive offices, participate in the China compliance subcommittee. This subcommittee is part of a structure of regionally, functionally, and industry-oriented subcommittees and task forces that are chaired by USTR staff and comprised of staff from a wide range of federal agencies. USTR assigns responsibilities for issue analysis to members of the appropriate staff subcommittee. Sometimes China-related trade issues are coordinated in other groups or at a higher level in the interagency structure process. For example, the intellectual property subcommittee took responsibility for some China WTO issues and coordinated its activities with the China WTO Compliance Subcommittee, according to USTR officials.

USTR's China WTO Compliance Subcommittee adopted an action plan with eight components at its inaugural meeting on December 4, 2001. The action plan had eight components. Under the plan, the subcommittee is to conduct

- comprehensive monitoring activities on a coordinated interagency basis, with input from private sector groups;

- regular dialogue with other WTO members;

- outreach to the private sector about the business environment it should expect in China;

- outreach to Chinese officials about their WTO commitments and compliance and its benefits;

- technical assistance and capacity building activities for China;

- active participation in the WTO Transitional Review Mechanism process;

---

[18]This subcommittee replaced an existing China subcommittee, which had a more general mandate and was not as active.

- facilitation of congressional oversight, by providing an annual report to Congress; and

- efforts to seek enforcement of U.S. rights through bilateral and multilateral means, including recourse to WTO dispute settlement procedures, as appropriate.

The China WTO Compliance Subcommittee was very active in its first year, and it met 11 times in 2002. In these meetings, officials evaluated and prioritized the monitoring activities undertaken, reviewed the steps that China has taken to implement its commitments, and decided on appropriate responses. Agency officials noted that much of the work and communication they do on China monitoring takes place informally outside of these formal meetings. Also, the subcommittee held a public hearing on September 18, 2002, and USTR issued its first annual report to Congress on China's WTO Compliance on December 11, 2002, as required by law.[19]

Still, it took some time for the subcommittee to get up to full speed. For example, it took time for the various participants to work out roles and responsibilities, according to some agency officials. USTR officials sought to delineate tasks related to carrying out their monitoring action plan in China, Washington, D.C., and Geneva, including expectations for information gathering, reporting, and setting initial priorities. Furthermore, agency officials told us that obtaining timely and accurate translations of Chinese laws and regulations was sometimes a problem, which affected the agencies' efforts to review the information. Also, agency officials undertook several activities at the beginning of the year to educate themselves on China's WTO obligations. This was important, because monitoring these obligations entailed new or expanded responsibilities for officials in the field and many of the Washington-based officials were relatively new to their current jobs. For example, many of the USTR officials who had actively participated in the U.S. negotiations with China establishing those obligations changed jobs and/or left the government soon after China became a WTO member in 2001. Nevertheless, monitoring activities took place throughout the entire year.

---

[19]Pub. L. 106-286, § 421, 114 Stat. 903.

| Informal Private Sector Participation Is Important to Monitoring | The private sector plays an important role in monitoring and enforcement activities. However, with regard to China, this role is generally carried out through informal contacts rather than through a formal system involving trade advisory committees from the private sector. These private sector committees complement the U.S. government's interagency committee system. |

USTR officials said the U.S. officials involved in China compliance monitoring obtain information from an informal, ad hoc network of business associations and individual companies to get information about Chinese trade practices and policies, to be alerted to market access problems and potential WTO violations, and to help weigh policy options. Business–government contacts take place both in China and in Washington, D.C. According to USTR officials, most of their business contacts are with individual companies. Business groups, including the U.S.-China Business Council, the U.S. Chamber of Commerce, the National Association of Manufacturers, and the American Chamber of Commerce in China, among others, also provide input and comment on policies relevant to the members of their organizations.

USTR officials said that USTR, Commerce, and USDA officials keep the various formal trade advisory committees informed of their China compliance-related activities and they sometimes receive input from these groups about the issues that concern them.[20] However, these committees are not the primary source of private sector involvement in China-related monitoring and enforcement. There is no active private sector advisory committee on China or any geographic area.[21]

A number of U.S. business and industry association representatives we interviewed generally thought they had established a good working

---

[20]Congress created the private sector advisory committee system to ensure that U.S. trade policy and negotiation objectives reflect U.S. commercial and economic interests. (See sec. 135 of the Trade Act of 1974, as amended, codified at 19 U.S.C. § 2155.) Generally, these advisory committees provide information and advice both prior to the United States entering into trade agreement negotiations and on other matters relating to U.S. trade policy. See U.S. General Accounting Office, *International Trade: Advisory Committee System Should Be Updated to Better Serve U.S. Policy Needs*, GAO-02-876 (Washington, D.C.: Sept. 24, 2002).

[21]Instead, the advisory committees that the agencies keep informed have an industry-specific or sector focus, such as on agricultural commodities or on functional cross-sectoral issues, such as intellectual property rights.

relationship with executive branch officials on China trade issues. In our 2002 survey of U.S. companies with a presence in China, we asked business representatives whom they would be likely to contact if faced with difficulties related to China's implementation of its WTO commitments. Business representatives reported that they were most likely to contact the U.S. embassy or consulate in China, their U.S. trade associations, China's Ministry of Foreign Trade and Economic Cooperation, and USTR. They were less likely to contact other U.S. agencies in Washington, D.C. (See table 2.)

Table 2: U.S. Company Likelihood of Contacting Groups Regarding Difficulties Related to China's Implementation of Its WTO Commitments

Contact groups (Rank-ordered responses expressed as percents)	Very or somewhat likely	Likely as unlikely	Very or somewhat unlikely	Don't know	Number of response
U.S. embassy or consulate in China	59%	10%	21%	9%	181
U.S. trade associations representing your company's interests	55	13	22	10	183
China's Ministry of Foreign Trade and Economic Cooperation	43	14	30	13	183
U.S. Trade Representative	42	21	25	12	178
Other Chinese government agencies or officials	40	12	21	28	165
Chinese consultants	39	16	34	12	178
WTO Center in Shanghai	38	17	28	17	177
U.S. Department of Commerce	36	21	30	13	179
U.S. Department of State	23	21	40	16	178
Other[a]	22	0	26	52	23
U.S. Congress	21	21	46	13	175
U.S. Department of Agriculture	8	13	64	15	172

Source: GAO.

Notes: GAO Survey of U.S. Companies on China-WTO issues, question 22 (reprinted in U.S. General Accounting Office, *World Trade Organization: Selected U.S. Company Views About China's Membership*, GAO-02-1056 [Washington, D.C.: Sept. 23, 2002], p. 46).

Percentages are based on the number of respondents answering each question item.

[a]Other responses included, among others, China's Ministry of Finance, U.S. Treasury, and the U.S.-China Business Council.

Companies reported mixed views regarding concerns that reporting compliance problems with WTO commitments to the U.S. government might result in retaliatory action by Chinese government entities against their companies. Specifically, almost half of the 48 companies that we interviewed said they were concerned about retaliatory action, and at least one had experienced such actions at first hand. A number of company representatives explained that they prefer to work under the cover of industry associations, resolve problems behind the scenes, and/or resolve problems directly in order to preserve business relationships in China. Other company representatives who did not fear retaliation noted that they had a history of raising issues with either the U.S. or the Chinese government.

U.S. Experience in Two Areas Illustrates Challenges Ahead

U.S. agencies' experiences in addressing compliance issues that arose in two areas during the first year of China's WTO membership illustrate the challenges ahead. First, problems regarding China's commitments to grant market access to certain bulk agricultural commodities through the use of tariff-rate quotas (TRQ) show the extensive effort that is needed to identify and begin to resolve what are sometimes complex and technical issues. Second, disagreement over implementing commitments creating a comprehensive review–referred to as a transitional review mechanism (TRM)–within the WTO to monitor China's compliance shows the importance of having common expectations and gaining early consensus on the meaning of the terms agreed upon in a multilateral forum. In both of these areas, we describe the relevant WTO commitments that China made, the issues that arose in 2002 regarding implementation of these commitments, and the ways in which U.S. agencies sought to resolve these issues. The problems in both of these areas are unresolved, and these areas illustrate the types of challenges that U.S. officials may face in the second year of China's membership. China's actions regarding the interpretation and implementation of these commitments provide insight into how China might act as a WTO member in the future with regard to contentious issues. U.S. officials plan to pursue resolution of the TRQ and TRM issues with China in 2003.

Agricultural TRQs Demonstrate Monitoring Challenges

China's implementation of its agricultural TRQ commitments was an area of contention in the first year of China's WTO membership. Under China's TRQ commitments, a specific quantity of certain agricultural bulk commodities is to be allowed in at a low duty, while imports above that quota amount face higher tariffs. The commodities covered by TRQs are sensitive to China, and the trading of these commodities has been under government control.[22] At the same time, these commodities are important for U.S. exporters because of the great market potential in China. According to USDA estimates, the increased access to China's market under the WTO will expand annual U.S. farm incomes by $800 million from 2002 to 2009. Notwithstanding the potential of China's market for agricultural goods, USTR highlighted agriculture as one of the three general areas (in addition to systemic transparency concerns) that generated significant problems in 2002 and warranted continued U.S. scrutiny. More specifically, USTR noted that the administration of China's TRQ system was the "most troublesome" area within agriculture. The issues surrounding China's implementation of its TRQ commitments are ongoing, and the problems have yet to be resolved. Meanwhile, the United States has attempted to resolve these problems through both bilateral and multilateral efforts.

China's Agricultural TRQ Commitments Are Detailed, Varied, and Numerous

China's commitments relating to agricultural TRQs are detailed, varied, and numerous. Some commitments provide specific procedural guidance for administering China's TRQ system, while others address the general principles of how the system should operate. China's administration of its TRQ system, which includes decisions about how much of the total quota amount for each product is allocated and to whom, affects whether exporters can take full advantage of the market potential in China. The large number and type of TRQ commitments reflect the concerns that some WTO members held about the way in which China's TRQ system would operate following its accession. For example, among the 58 WTO commitments that we identified as relating to TRQs, we found 40 to be guidance related. These types of commitments provide specific procedures for how China should administer its TRQ system. However, some commitments are less specific, such as those that address the general principles that China should abide by. China has committed to

---

[22]These agricultural bulk commodities include wheat, corn, rice, cotton, soybean oil, palm oil, rapeseed oil, sugar, and wool, covering 37 tariff lines in China's WTO accession schedule.

- increase its tariff-rate quota volumes over a 3 to 4 year implementation period;

- reserve a portion of the TRQs for importation through trading enterprises not run by the government;

- administer TRQs on a transparent, predictable, uniform, fair, and nondiscriminatory basis;

- follow specific time lines to publish quotas, accept applications, and allocate TRQs;

- establish government enquiry points and publish information on its quota allocation in an official journal; and

- designate a single, central authority to make the decisions regarding all allocations and reallocations to end-users.

TRQ Implementation Issues Ranged Widely

Besides a cross-cutting U.S. concern over transparency, a wide range of issues relating to China's TRQ administration caused concern in the first year of China's membership.[23] Examples of the issues include the following: (1) China's quota allocations to end-users missed the deadlines specified in the commitments; (2) the United States and China presented different opinions on what constitutes a "commercially viable" shipping quantity; and (3) the United States and China disagreed on whether China's reserving a portion of the TRQ for reexporting violated China's WTO commitments.

First, China missed the deadline specified in the accession agreement for issuing the quotas. China's designated authority for agricultural TRQ administration, SDPC, was late to issue both draft and final regulations on TRQ quota allocation. Not only was SDPC late to begin the TRQ quota application process, but also its subsequent allocation of TRQs did not begin until late April 2002, approximately 4 months after the date specified in China's WTO commitments. U.S. officials were unsure of the precise effect of this delay on market access. However, they agreed that the delay

---

[23]USTR pointed out that China's designated TRQ administrative authority, the State Development and Planning Commission (SDPC), offered limited transparency, because the authority refused to provide specific details on the amounts and the recipients of the TRQ allocations.

probably reduced the benefit of the quota allocations in 2002, since U.S. exporters missed the spring marketing season. Chinese officials whom we interviewed outlined several reasons for the delay: (1) China received many more applications for TRQs than expected, thus placing a heavy burden on China's limited resources; (2) the switch of TRQ allocation authority from the provinces to a single central authority was a drastic adjustment for SDPC; and (3) China became a WTO member late in the year and therefore did not have enough time to prepare to issue TRQs by January 1. Problems with the timeliness of TRQ allocations for certain of the commodities have surfaced in 2003 as well. According to USTR and USDA officials, although China announced the 2003 TRQ amounts on time, the actual quota allocations to end-users had yet to be verified as of early March 2003.

Second, the United States and China presented different opinions on what constitutes commercially viable quantities. China's WTO commitments require that quotas be allocated in commercially viable shipping quantities. The United States believed that SDPC allocated a portion of its 2002 TRQs for some commodities in smaller than commercially viable quantities--that is, the amount of the quota was too small to justify the cost of shipping the product from the United States to China. China maintained that the allocations were in fact made in commercially viable quantities. However, China noted in the WTO Committee on Agriculture transitional review meeting in September 2002 that China was open to considering suggestions and further discussing this issue with the United States and other interested WTO members.

Third, the United States considered China's practice of reserving a portion of the quotas for "processing trade" to be inconsistent with WTO obligations. China reserved a certain portion of the TRQ for each agricultural commodity for companies that process the imported commodities for reexport. End-users that received such quota allocations (after applying to another ministry) were required to reexport the processed product, and selling of the processed product in the Chinese domestic market was prohibited. In its first-year compliance report, USTR argued that this practice limited the market share held by foreign imports in China's domestic markets. At the same time, they contended that this practice distorted trade by creating greater competition for WTO members' processed goods in export markets outside of China. The United States further argued against the practice of reserving a portion of the TRQ for processing trade by referring to other commitments China had made as well as to general WTO principles.[24] China responded that the processing trade has been in existence for 2 decades and that many enterprises in China, including joint ventures, engage in this business. China argued that those business interests should be accommodated. Furthermore, reserving a portion of the TRQs for those enterprises was based on objective demand and consumer preferences, and thus the practice was within the framework of TRQ commitments.

United States Used Multiple Sources and Bilateral and Multilateral Means to Address TRQ Issues

The U.S. experience in addressing TRQ issues in 2002 shows that monitoring China's compliance can entail significant effort. U.S. government agencies gathered information from the private sector, U.S. embassy personnel, and the Chinese government to identify potential problems concerning China's compliance with its TRQ commitments. First, U.S. agencies used an informal network of business associations and individual companies to obtain information about Chinese trade practices and policies and to be alerted to market access problems and potential WTO violations. Industry groups used formal and informal channels to voice their concerns over TRQ implementation and provided input for USTR's comments to the Chinese government on TRQ regulations. Several agricultural groups and companies also submitted written comments for USTR's report on China's WTO compliance in September 2002. Agricultural

---

[24]Among others, some of the arguments the U.S. made against China's practice are the following: (1) The practice lacks transparency; (2) The practice appears to be inconsistent with China's obligation to have a single, central authority (SDPC) to administer TRQs; (3) The practice appears to be inconsistent with the obligation to allocate the entire TRQ to end-users by January 1 of each year; and (4) The practice improperly attaches restrictions to the use of some imported products.

groups we interviewed noted that they also relied on informal means to communicate with USTR and USDA. Second, agency officials working in the U.S. embassy in Beijing were another prominent source of information. For example, the U.S. embassy translated various TRQ regulations from Chinese to English. The third source of information was the Chinese government. SDPC circulated the interim regulation on TRQs and the allocation guidance for public comment before issuing them in final form. USTR, USDA, and other agencies in the interagency process analyzed this information and determined how to respond. Therefore, USTR was able to provide detailed written feedback to the Chinese and anticipate potential problems. For example, the U.S. concern over reserving a portion of the quotas for the processing trade was expressed in the U.S. comments on the draft regulations early in the process of responding to China's TRQ administration.

In responding to the TRQ compliance problems, the U.S. government used both bilateral and multilateral mechanisms. The bilateral activities included sending a "demarche," or formal message, and letters to Chinese officials. Additionally, TRQs were discussed during USTR, USDA, State, and Commerce officials' visits to China throughout the year. However, early bilateral meetings with the Chinese did not enable the United States to obtain the information it was seeking. So, after an interagency decision, the United States invoked a Chinese commitment for more formal bilateral consultations at the WTO. As a result of those consultations, the United States was able to get additional information about China's TRQ administration. Generally, the United States tried to engage other WTO members to help resolve problems with China if there was multilateral interest. Additionally, five WTO members submitted questions to China relating to TRQs in the context of the transitional review mechanism at the WTO in September. The time line in table 3 illustrates the considerable number and type of activities that U.S. officials undertook at the bilateral and WTO multilateral level from late 2001 to early 2003 to address TRQ issues.

Table 3: Time line of Key U.S. Government TRQ-Related Activities and Events, 2001-2003

Date	Bilateral activities and events	WTO multilateral activities and events
November 2001	U.S. provides written comments to China on draft TRQ regulations.	
December	USTR Chief Agricultural Negotiator meets with SDPC to discuss timeliness and other concerns related to TRQs.	USTR raises TRQ concerns with Chinese representative on the margins of the WTO General Council meeting.
January 2002	Demarche notes China's failure to publish regulations and application criteria, as well as allocate quotas by Jan. 1, 2002.	
February	U.S. provides written comments to China on final TRQ regulations. U.S. delegation raises agriculture-related concerns, including TRQs, during Bush-Jiang summit in Beijing. Demarche encourages China to allocate TRQs and publish relevant information as soon as possible.	
March	USTR official meets with MOFTEC officials about TRQ concerns.	U.S. delegation attends special session of the Committee on Agriculture and raises China TRQ issue.
April	USTR Ambassador raises TRQ issues during visit to China. Subsequently, raises TRQ issues again in follow-up letter to MOFTEC Minister. Commerce Undersecretary meets with Chinese officials and is told that the national government has forwarded information on TRQs to the provinces. Commerce Secretary raises TRQ issues during visit to China. USTR officials meet with Chinese officials and are reassured of the allocation of TRQs. Demarche encourages the Chinese to make TRQ allocations. U.S. embassy requests a list of recipients for TRQ allocations from SDPC and MOFTEC.	
May	Demarche requests information about the TRQ allocations and expresses concern over lack of response from China on earlier requests. USTR Ambassador raises TRQ issues with MOFTEC Minister at Asia Pacific Economic Cooperation Ministerial.	U.S. addresses TRQ issues at the meeting of the Committee on Import Licensing. China responds that it has not anticipated difficulty and promises to allocate on time next year.
June	Demarche requests that Chinese officials take responsibility for TRQ allocation. SDPC official meets with USTR official to discuss the status of China's TRQ allocations.	U.S. raises TRQ issues at WTO Market Access Committee meeting. U.S. raises TRQ issues at WTO Agriculture Committee meeting.

(Continued From Previous Page)

Date	Bilateral activities and events	WTO multilateral activities and events
July	USTR official meets with Chinese officials to discuss TRQ allocations. Commerce official meets with MOFTEC officials to discuss TRQ concerns.	USTR formally requests bilateral consultation with China in Geneva concerning TRQ administration of agricultural goods for August 12, 2002.
August	Letter from USDA to Chinese official notes the need to address the TRQ problem. USDA Secretary discusses TRQ issues during visit to China.	
September	An interagency team lead by USTR has discussions with senior Chinese officials in Beijing in a lead-up to the Crawford, Texas Presidential Summit.	USTR holds formal consultations (under the TRQ headnote) in Geneva with a delegation from China. Committee on Agriculture holds its 32nd meeting on September 26. China responds to questions and comments regarding TRQs by the United States, Canada, the European Community, Japan, and Thailand in advance of the review. U.S. raises TRQ issues at WTO Market Access Committee transitional review meeting. U.S. raises TRQ issues at WTO Import Licensing Committee transitional review meeting.
October	FAS letter to SDPC delineates various concerns regarding TRQ implementation.	
November		U.S. delegation asks China about the TRQ license application process and the requirement that China has set aside a portion of the TRQ for entities that further process and/or reexport product imported under the TRQ at the WTO Committee on Agriculture meeting in Geneva.
December	USTR sends letter to MOFTEC concerning China's TRQ administration of bulk agricultural products.	
January 2003		USTR meets with Chinese delegation to the WTO in Geneva to lay the groundwork for USTR Ambassador's trip to China and to discuss TRQ implementation issues.
February 2003	USTR Ambassador meets with Chinese Premier-elect and MOFTEC Minister and discusses TRQs. Deputy USTR raises TRQ concerns during new trade dialog in Beijing.	

Source: USTR, USDA, Commerce, and State.

Note: MOFTEC = Ministry of Foreign Trade and Economic Cooperation.

GAO-03-461 Monitoring China's WTO Compliance

TRQ Issues Are Still Ongoing, as Private Sector Concerns Continue

U.S. officials continue to pursue many of the TRQ-related issues with China to gain greater market access for U.S. exports of the affected products. In a December 2002 letter, the National Cotton Council urged the U.S. government to initiate dispute settlement consultations in the WTO with respect to China's implementation of its TRQ for imported cotton fiber, and, if necessary, request the establishment of a dispute settlement panel to resolve the issue. It is important to note that implementation problems are not universal across all commodities. For example, getting a list of TRQ quota holders and a commercially viable shipping quantity have been concerns for U.S. cotton exporters but not for U.S. exporters of edible oil, according to industry representatives we interviewed. Furthermore, the various U.S. agricultural groups' level of concern over China's TRQ implementation varies because the commercial considerations vary for each commodity. China's administration of its TRQ system is only one among many factors that affect U.S. exports to China. Chinese domestic demand and supply, as well as the size of the domestic Chinese stock of these commodities are important determinants of trade flows. Also, international competition with other exporting countries as well as exchange rates affect U.S. exports to China. As a result of all these factors together, in 2002, the level of agricultural exports that filled the various Chinese quota amounts for the TRQ commodities ranged from zero to 67 percent.[25]

---

[25]The percentage of China's TRQs that were actually filled (that is, fill rate) in 2002 for certain key commodities including corn was 0.1 percent; cotton, 21.6 percent; soybean oil, 34.6 percent; sugar, 67.1 percent; and wheat 7.5 percent. The simple average of the TRQ fill rate for all countries reported by WTO was 50 percent in 1999.

The Transitional Review Mechanism Did Not Meet U.S. Expectations

Because China's economy is in a transitional stage from a nonmarket to a market economy, and because China's commitments required China to make extensive changes to its trade regime, WTO members, and particularly the United States,[26] pushed for China's accession package to include commitments creating a transitional review mechanism. This mechanism is intended to be a means for WTO members to annually review China's implementation of its WTO commitments and the development of China's trade with other WTO members until all of China's commitments are phased in.[27] These TRM commitments are important, because they establish a multilateral monitoring mechanism that allows WTO members to better understand China's trade practices and to communicate their expectations to China.

Just as the establishment of a transitional review mechanism was one of the more challenging issues to negotiate with China, implementing the process during the first year (2002) also proved to be challenging. WTO members did not reach consensus on how the review should proceed because of the lack of specificity in some of the commitments, leaving the process open to debate. The United States, China, and other WTO members had different expectations about what the review should entail and produce. They disagreed on the form and timing of the information to be exchanged and on the thoroughness of the review. U.S. activities to resolve these differences on a multilateral basis through the WTO did not yield a consensus and were unsuccessful. As a result, with few exceptions, there was not a complete and thorough review of China's compliance issues, nor any summary conclusions about the first year of China's implementation by the WTO. Thus, the TRM process fell short of the meaningful review hoped for by U.S. and other country officials. U.S. government officials agreed that the TRM process would have worked better if there had been greater consensus from WTO members on their expectations regarding China's actions. However, U.S. officials cited benefits from participating in the TRM process, such as demonstrating to China the United States' commitment to

---

[26]A provision in the legislation authorizing the President to grant permanent normal trade relations to China stated that "[i]t shall be the objective of the United States to obtain. . .an annual review within the WTO of the compliance by the People's Republic of China with its terms of accession to the WTO" (Pub.L. 106-286, § 401, 114 Stat. 900).

[27]The TRM is additional to the WTO's trade policy review mechanism, which provides for a broad review of the trade regimes of all WTO members on a scheduled basis. However, WTO members viewed the trade policy review mechanism as insufficient to oversee China's implementation of its commitments and pursued the TRM.

thoroughly reviewing China's WTO implementation, and solidifying interagency coordination for the years ahead. U.S. officials said they are hopeful that they can work with China and other WTO members to achieve more workable procedures for future reviews.

Commitments Create TRM, but Procedural Details Not Specified

The transitional review mechanism, which is unique to China, is defined through about 75 commitments in China's accession agreement.[28] The commitments address two matters: (1) the scope and process for the WTO review and (2) the exchange of information. First, these TRM commitments lay out the scope of review and some procedures for China and WTO members to follow. About a dozen commitments require annual reviews by all 16 WTO subsidiary bodies and then by the WTO General Council, making use of the results of those of the subsidiary bodies.[29] The reviews are to occur annually for 8 years, with a final review in year 10.[30] The General Council reviews are not limited to an examination of China's implementation of its WTO commitments but are to include broader issues dealing with (1) the development of China's trade with WTO members and other trading partners and (2) recent developments and cross-sectoral issues regarding China's trade regime. Second, in regard to the exchange of information, China's accession agreement sets forth a broad range of information that China must provide annually to the 16 WTO subsidiary bodies for their reviews. We identified 62 commitments requiring China to provide economic data and information on its (1) economic policies, (2) framework for making and enforcing policies, (3) policies affecting trade in goods and services, and (4) trade-related intellectual property regime.

USTR officials believed additional rules were needed to ensure timely responses from China. While China's accession agreement establishes a general framework for TRM procedures, several other aspects of the

---

[28]For more details regarding how we analyzed the commitments, see U.S. General Accounting Office, *World Trade Organization: Analysis of China's Commitments to Other Members*, GAO-03-4 (Washington, D.C.: Oct. 3, 2002).

[29]The General Council is composed of all WTO members and has general authority to supervise the various agreements under the jurisdiction of the WTO. The subsidiary bodies are described as councils or committees and generally are organized according to the various trade subjects covered by the WTO agreements–for example, the Council for Trade in Goods, the Council for Trade in Services, and the Committees on Agriculture and Technical Barriers to Trade.

[30]The agreement does not specifically say when the reviews will end. Although the review process is scheduled to conclude with a final review in the 10th year after China's accession, the General Council could decide to terminate it at any time after the 8th year.

review are not specified. Therefore, these aspects have to be coordinated between the members of the various WTO subsidiary bodies and the General Council, which includes China. For example, China's commitments require China to submit information and documentation relating to the General Council's review no later than 30 days prior to the review date. However, there is no similar specific requirement for when China needs to provide information to the subsidiary bodies for their reviews, which need to be done before those of the General Council. Similarly, China is to respond to specific questions from members in connection with the review conducted by both the subsidiary bodies and the General Council. However, while the agreement indicates that members should submit questions and China should respond to those questions in advance of the reviews, the agreement does not establish how the process should work with any more particularity. For example, the agreement does not set forth agreed timelines for the process, nor whether questions raised in advance by WTO members should be answered in writing or provided orally.

No Consensus on Expectations for TRM

U.S. officials expected a detailed multilateral review of China's WTO implementation each year of the TRM, but this expectation differed from that of China. Under U.S. expectations, China's TRM would follow a set of mutually agreed to procedures, and China would provide the usual information required of all WTO members as well as additional information related to its accession agreement. Furthermore, U.S. officials expected that China would respond to their questions before the relevant WTO committee meetings and in writing. They also expected opportunities for follow-up questions and answers either in writing or in subsequent meetings. With all this information in hand, members then could thoroughly analyze the answers and take them into account as part of their review to come to conclusions about China's implementation. In addition, U.S. officials initially were seeking to have the WTO General Council synthesize the results of the reports of the various subsidiary bodies, come to some summary conclusions, and issue a final report with recommendations.

Chinese officials seemed to expect a more limited review and took a more narrow view of the TRM commitments. In fact, Chinese officials told us that while they would abide by these commitments, they considered the review mechanism discriminatory in nature, since it only applied to China, and that it had been "imposed on them." They would not accept any additional procedures concerning the form, nature, and timing of the information they were to submit or the review itself. Chinese officials told us that such procedures were not in the commitments and appeared to them as an attempt to renegotiate and add to the terms of their accession. They took the position that any information that was specifically called for in their commitments (outside of regular WTO notification requirements) could be submitted orally and that it need not be submitted before individual committee meetings where the "review" was to take place. Chinese officials believed the review should come at the last meeting of the year in each subsidiary body, just before the last General Council meeting in 2002, and should be limited to that one meeting.

The expectations of other WTO members varied. Some members sympathized with China and believed that other WTO members were pushing the TRM too hard, especially since this was the first year of China's membership. Other members were less sympathetic and expected the review to help resolve problems and to exert pressure on China to fully implement its commitments. Similarly, there was no agreement among WTO members concerning the interpretation and implementation of the TRM commitments. For example, some members agreed with China and did not think that these commitments required China to answer questions in writing and did not expect China to do so. Other members shared the U.S. expectation that Chinese commitments to provide information to other members in advance implicitly required China to provide answers in writing. Additionally, other members' expectations about the nature of the final product of the review also varied or were uncertain.

U.S. Activities Related to TRM Implementation

Planning and preparations for the first WTO review of China's implementation of its commitments got off to a slow start after China became a WTO member. Through the first half of 2002, U.S. officials, other WTO members, and WTO Secretariat officials searched for consensus about how the review should proceed. Moreover, there was a lack of an early plan of action from the United States, other WTO members, and the WTO Secretariat[31] concerning scheduling meetings and other procedural issues. Chinese officials refused to agree to have any discussion of TRM-related procedures placed on the agenda for (early) subsidiary body meetings. At that time, officials from other member countries expressed concern that the lack of an agreed strategy on TRM procedures might affect the quality of the reviews.

---

[31]The WTO Secretariat's main duties are to supply technical support for the various councils and committees and the ministerial conferences, to provide technical assistance for developing countries, to analyze world trade, and to explain WTO affairs to the public and the media.

It was not until April 2002 that the U.S. interagency China WTO Compliance Subcommittee agreed to a paper for the WTO setting forth U.S. views as to the appropriate timing and procedures for the TRM. The United States proposed that China submit the information called for in its accession agreement and that members' questions and China's answers begin to be exchanged in writing at agreed time periods in advance of each subsidiary body meeting so that further exchanges could take place at the meetings themselves. Furthermore, the United States proposed that the required WTO reports present a focused juxtaposition of members' concerns and Chinese responses. U.S. officials said they were open to other procedures that accomplished their objectives.

However, Chinese officials rejected the U.S. proposal and any deadlines and requests for written answers to members' questions. USTR held formal and informal discussions in Geneva to resolve the various logistical matters and procedures necessary to implement the TRM properly, such as the dates of meetings and the deadlines for China to submit relevant information and to respond to other WTO members' questions. USTR said that these discussions had not gone as quickly as it would have liked, in part because the Chinese delegation was still trying to become familiar with WTO practices and procedures. Around midyear, it was accepted that the TRM would begin with WTO subsidiary body meetings in September, according to USTR officials.

Thus, with regard to the TRM, U.S. activities in the first half of 2002 were focused on procedural issues. With no consensus on the TRM, each subsidiary body made ad hoc decisions about how the TRM would proceed, according to USTR officials.

Nevertheless, beginning in March the U.S. and other WTO member officials began raising individual substantive implementation issues with Chinese officials on numerous occasions during various WTO meetings. Typically these issues involved time-sensitive matters, for which it did not make sense to wait for the annual TRM in the fall, according to USTR officials.

Then in the second half of 2002, U.S. activities focused on raising substantive issues in the TRM context. In July, USTR began preparations for U.S. participation in the TRM, establishing deadlines for the U.S. agencies comprising the China WTO Compliance Subcommittee to provide input for questions to ask China in advance of the WTO subsidiary body reviews. USTR also solicited the views of the private sector through the chairs of the various formal trade advisory committees. The United States and other WTO members submitted questions in writing to the Chinese in advance and tried to press them for further information during various committee meetings. Table 4 presents a chronology of key events related to the TRM in 2002.

Table 4: Time line of Key TRM-related Activities and Events, 2002

Month	Event
January	
February	
March	U.S. interagency China WTO Compliance Subcommittee discusses TRM.
April	China WTO Compliance Subcommittee approves U.S. proposal on TRM timing and procedures.
	China blocks TRM from being placed on some committee agendas. China rejects U.S. proposal.
May	USTR holds bilateral consultations with Chinese and other WTO members on TRM procedures.
June	USTR holds bilateral consultations with Chinese and other WTO members on TRM procedures.
July	USTR requests input on TRM from Interagency Trade Advisory Committees and Private Sector Trade Advisors on behalf of the China WTO Compliance Subcommittee.
August	United States begins submitting written questions to China for TRM issues in advance of subsidiary body meetings.
September	Review by Council on TRIPS, and committees on Agriculture, Antidumping, Import Licensing, and Market Access.
October	Review by Council on Services, and committees on Technical Barriers to Trade, Safeguards, Trade-Related Investment Measures, and Financial Services.
November	Review by Council on Goods and committees on Balance-of-Payments, Sanitary and Phytosanitary Measures, Subsidies, Customs Valuation, and Rules of Origin.
December	Review by General Council.

Source: USTR and WTO documents.

Note: TRIPS = Trade-Related Aspects of Intellectual Property Rights.

WTO Review Was Limited and Results Were Disappointing

The depth of the TRM reviews conducted in almost all the reviewing WTO councils and committees was limited. Overall, the Chinese did an adequate job of submitting their standard written WTO notifications and other information called for in China's accession agreement, according to USTR officials. However, in several committee meetings, U.S. officials expressed their disappointment that China missed deadlines, provided incomplete information, and failed to meet some reporting requirements. While the United States and other WTO members sought answers to their questions in writing well before WTO meetings, Chinese officials submitted answers to some questions in writing just before or during meetings and submitted written versions of their oral answers to other members' questions after some other meetings. While appreciating the answers they received, some WTO members expressed concern in many meetings that all of their questions had not been fully answered. In response, Chinese officials offered to give information to individual members bilaterally and orally after the meetings but outside of the context of the TRM. Although China's WTO "notifications" containing the usual information required of all WTO members were useful, U.S. officials did not obtain the type of additional information they had hoped for. A USTR official said that the method of operation that the WTO eventually adopted for the first year was an interim solution that needs to be improved upon.

Generally, however, U.S. officials told us they were disappointed with the results of the first TRM. The subsidiary bodies held their reviews in September through November 2002 and did not conduct any assessment per se. The reports to the General Council were factual and limited to descriptions of the discussion in the meetings where the review was held; these descriptions presented the issues that WTO members raised and China's responses in the meetings without providing any summary, analysis, or conclusions. The General Council held its review in December; however, it did not issue a report and it did not make any recommendations.

Other WTO members recognized that the 2002 TRM process had problems as well. Several WTO members expressed frustration in some WTO subsidiary body meetings about the TRM and said they were not satisfied with the review that had taken place. During the General Council review, several WTO members, including the United States, expressed hope that the TRM process could be improved in 2003. Acknowledging the problems in the 2002 review overall, the Chairman of the General Council said that next year's TRM would benefit from having time built into the process throughout the year to conduct the next review.

U.S. Officials Noted Some Benefits of TRM

While U.S. officials recognized that there were many problems in the WTO's review of China's compliance under the TRM process in 2002, they said that the effort was valuable nevertheless. First, the process enabled them to have a constant engagement with China on a wide variety of issues—in a multilateral setting. As a result, the United States was able to demonstrate to China its commitment to reviewing China's WTO implementation. Second, as part of the process there was a greater flow of information— between WTO members and China, and also within national bureaucracies. Third, the process further institutionalized China's commitment to reform.

Furthermore, U.S. officials told us that the U.S. government's monitoring efforts benefited at the interagency level from the experience gained in participating in the TRM process. For example, some officials noted that the TRM resulted in improved U.S. government attention to China WTO compliance issues. The process also forced better coordination and cooperation among agencies as they worked together to submit questions and analysis to Geneva in advance of the WTO committee meetings.

Implications for the 2003 Review

The first year of China's TRM did not result in the thorough and detailed multilateral review of China's compliance that U.S. officials envisioned. If the experience in the 2002 TRM does not result in improvements, however, the situation could set an unfortunate precedent for future WTO reviews of China. While the review was beneficial, it was undercut by the U.S. and other WTO members' inability to get complete and timely information from China and by disagreement over whether the WTO should come to any conclusions or make any recommendations about China's implementation of its WTO commitments. It is important to acknowledge two mitigating factors. First, this was the first year of operations for the TRM and the China WTO Compliance Subcommittee that coordinates U.S. participation. Second, any changes in the WTO review process would have required the consensus of all members, including the Chinese. The incentives for China to do so are unclear. Nevertheless, without any change, continued problems and frustrations can be expected as a result of the 2003 review.

However, USTR officials told us they would continue to press for procedures that will provide for the orderly give and take of information. For example, they said they could build on the relatively successful 2002 review in the Council on Trade-Related Aspects of Intellectual Property Rights, which reviewed implementation of China's legislation in this area. USTR officials told us they plan to consult with other WTO members about how to improve the TRM through more regular procedures. They hope that more countries will actively participate in the next review, since only a handful of countries submitted questions in advance of subsidiary body meetings in 2002. USTR officials told us that they have begun to develop a strategy to make the process better for the future, and they raised the issue with Chinese officials in February 2003. They are optimistic that China will be more open to multilateral review of its compliance now that it has the experience of being a WTO member for more than 1 year.

Agency Comments and Our Evaluation

We requested comments on a draft of this report from the U.S. Trade Representative and the secretaries of Agriculture, Commerce, and State or his or her designee. On March 18, 2003, the Deputy Assistant U.S. Trade Representative for China provided us with written technical comments on the draft. These comments included the views of officials from the departments of Commerce and State, which were transmitted to USTR in its capacity as chair of the interagency Trade Policy Staff Committee, Subcommittee on China WTO Compliance. Department of Agriculture officials provided written comments directly to us on March 17, 2003.

Many of the agency officials' comments focused on our in-depth look at TRQ and TRM issues. USTR officials provided us new information about additional key efforts they had made to resolve the TRQ problem "in order to give a proper sense of what is involved in pressing sensitive issues like TRQs," and we incorporated this information in the draft report where appropriate. We also revised the draft based on technical comments regarding our descriptions of first-year TRQ compliance issues and the status of China's TRQ allocations in 2003. In response to their comments on our draft TRM section, we clarified our observation that it was planning and preparations for the TRM that got off to a slow start, not the WTO TRM process itself, which was expected to begin in the fall, according to USTR officials. Furthermore, we clarified our description of the United States and other members raising questions about China's WTO implementation to make it apparent that these efforts began earlier in the year and were independent of the transitional review for China. We made similar clarifications to this section about the consensus needed to proceed in the WTO and the benefits of the first TRM, among other things. We also modified our observations about the U.S. government's preparations for the 2003 TRM after USTR officials provided some additional information about their plans and activities to date.

Agency officials also made specific technical and editorial comments about other sections of the draft, which we accepted when appropriate. For example, we made changes to the draft regarding our discussion of agency resources based on State's estimates of full-time equivalent staff in the Beijing embassy's economic section working on China compliance issues. In some cases we declined to accept the agencies' alternative characterizations. For example, the agencies disagreed with our observation that it took some time for interagency roles and responsibilities to be worked out. They commented that this was a relatively short period of time and that such a situation might be expected with a new endeavor of this type. While we present the agencies' comment here, we nevertheless believe that it is important to make it clear that there were some initial difficulties associated with interagency coordination on China WTO compliance during 2002.

We are sending copies of this report to the U.S. Trade Representative, the secretaries of Agriculture, Commerce, and State, and interested congressional committees. Copies of this report will also be made available to other interested parties on request. In addition, the report will be made available at no charge on the GAO Web site at http://www.gao.gov.

If you or your staff have any questions about this report, please contact me on (202) 512-4128. Other GAO contacts and staff acknowledgments are listed in appendix II.

Susan S. Westin

Susan S. Westin
Managing Director
International Affairs and Trade

Objectives, Scope, and Methodology

As part of a long-term body of work that the Chairman and the Ranking Minority Member of the Senate Committee on Finance, as well as the Chairman and the Ranking Minority Member of the House Committee on Ways and Means, requested, we examined how the U.S. Trade Representative (USTR) and the departments of Commerce, Agriculture (USDA), and State are positioned to monitor and enforce China's compliance with its World Trade Organization (WTO) commitments. Specifically, in this report, we (1) describe the changes to each agency's plans, organization, and resources in light of China's accession to the WTO, and to the interagency process used to fulfill these responsibilities; and (2) review how these agencies have addressed certain compliance issues that have arisen during the first year of China's WTO membership.

To describe the changes to the agencies' organization, resources, and plans, and to the interagency process used to monitor and enforce China's compliance, we reviewed a variety of official documents and interviewed knowledgeable agency officials. First, we reviewed each agency's most recent performance and strategic plans to determine how China WTO monitoring and enforcement is incorporated into the agencies' planning processes. Second, to determine how each agency is organized to carry out China WTO compliance efforts, we reviewed official statements and other agency documents, including information that describes the structure and function of intra-agency China WTO compliance teams. We supplemented this information by interviewing knowledgeable agency officials. Third, we asked each agency to provide us with the actual number of full-time equivalent staff in key units involved in China WTO compliance efforts for fiscal years 2000 to 2002. If detailed staffing data were not available, we asked the agency to estimate the number of actual full-time equivalent staff involved in the agency's China WTO compliance activities. We did not verify the accuracy of the agencies' estimates. Last, we reviewed documents detailing the interagency process for monitoring China's WTO compliance, including minutes, agendas, hearing submissions, and hearing transcripts from the Trade Policy Staff Committee, Subcommittee on China WTO Compliance.

To describe the role of the private sector, we interviewed several business associations, including the U.S.-China Business Council, the U.S. Chamber of Commerce, the National Association of Manufacturers, and the American Chamber of Commerce in China (Beijing and Shanghai). To determine where U.S. companies with a presence in China go for assistance with their compliance problems, we surveyed 551 selected chief executive officers or presidents of U.S. companies with a presence in China. We also conducted structured interviews with representatives of 48 U.S. firms in Beijing, Guangzhou, Shanghai, and Shenzhen, China.[1]

To review how these agencies have addressed compliance issues that have arisen in the first year of China's WTO membership, we examined two areas of China's commitments where there was significant monitoring and enforcement activity. First, we chose to examine activities related to China's regulating imports of certain bulk agricultural commodities through a tariff-rate quota (TRQ) system because (1) the area was economically important to U.S. exporters, (2) China made numerous WTO commitments to change its practices in this area, and (3) there was significant compliance activity on the part of the U.S. government in the first year of China's WTO membership related to this issue. Additionally, USTR noted that agriculture, and specifically China's regulation of these bulk commodities, was an area of concern for the first year of China's implementation of its WTO commitments. Second, we chose to examine activities that related to implementing an annual review—referred to as a transitional review mechanism (TRM)— of China's trade policies within the WTO, because the mechanism is an important aspect of WTO members' ability to monitor China's compliance with its commitments. Additionally, although the United States and some WTO members had problems with China's compliance with its TRM commitments, USTR did not discuss the issue in its first report to Congress on China's WTO compliance. Last, the area concerned issues that were important to Congress and other U.S. officials. For example, legislation authorizing the President to grant China permanent normal trade relations with the United States emphasized the importance of creating a multilateral review of China's commitments within the WTO by making the establishment of the review an explicit U.S. negotiating objective.[2] Our descriptions of China's commitments in these areas are based on our past work.[3]

It is important to note that these two areas are not representative of China's compliance record overall but do illustrate the kinds of compliance issues

---

[1]See U.S. General Accounting Office, *World Trade Organization: Selected Company Views About China's Membership*, GAO-02-1056 (Washington, D.C.: Sept. 23, 2002) for additional detail regarding our survey and structured interviews.

[2]Pub. L. 106-286, § 401, 114 Stat. 900.

[3]See U.S. General Accounting Office, *World Trade Organization: Analysis of China's Commitments to Other Members*, GAO-03-4 (Washington, D.C.: Oct. 3, 2002).

that U.S. officials try to resolve. Similarly, our observations about the U.S. government's experience in monitoring and enforcing commitments in these two areas cannot be generalized to other parts of the agreement. USTR's first report to Congress on China's WTO compliance described other examples of issues faced in the first year of China's membership.[4] The report noted that overall in 2002 China made significant progress in implementing its commitments, both in undertaking many of the required systemic changes and in implementing specific commitments. At the same time, the report noted serious concerns in some areas where implementation had not yet occurred or was inadequate.

To review TRQ issues, we analyzed WTO correspondence, U.S. government demarches and letters to Chinese officials, and questions from WTO members to China in the context of the TRM. In addition, we interviewed officials at the National Cotton Council of America, National Oilseed Processors Association, and U.S. Wheat Associates, and reviewed trade data related to these commodities.

To review issues related to the WTO's TRM for China, we analyzed World Trade Organization and U.S. agency documents, including summaries of questions submitted to the WTO's General Council and subsidiary committees, and interviewed knowledgeable U.S. government, foreign government, and World Trade Organization officials.

We performed our work from November 2002 through February 2003 in accordance with generally accepted government auditing standards. This work builds on prior GAO analyses initiated in July 2001.

---

[4]See U.S. Trade Representative, *2002 Report to Congress on China's WTO Compliance* (Washington, D.C.: Office of the U.S. Trade Representative, Dec. 11, 2002).

GAO Contacts and Staff Acknowledgments

GAO Contacts

Loren Yager (202) 512-5351
Adam Cowles (202) 512-9637
Matthew E. Helm (202) 512-7959

Acknowledgments

In addition to those named above, Ming Chen, Shakira Edwards, Nima Patel-Edwards, Jane-yu Li, Rona Mendelsohn, Michelle Sager, and Richard Seldin made key contributions to this report.

United States
General Accounting Office
Washington, D.C. 20548-0001

Official Business
Penalty for Private Use $300

Address Service Requested